DESERT
ANIMALS
Searchin'
for Shade

Bobcat

by Meish Goldish

Consultant:

Linda Searles, Executive Director
Southwest Wildlife Conservation Center
Scottsdale, Arizona

BEARPORT
PUBLISHING

New York, New York

Credits
Cover, © J&C Sohns/imageBROKER/Corbis; TOC, © Renee Lynn/Corbis; 4, © Anton Foltin/Shutterstock; 5, © Susan & Neil Silverma; 5T, © J&C Sohns; 7, © Associated Press; 8, © Design Pics Inc./Alamy; 9TL, © Sanne vd Berg Fotografie/Shutterstock; 9TR, © Fremme/Shutterstock; 9BL, © Arto Hakola/Shutterstock; 9BM, © Wayne Lynch; 9BR, © IrinaK/Shutterstock; 10, © Mary Ann McDonald/Corbis; 11, © Joel Sartore/National Geographic Creative; 12–13, © J&C Sohns/imageBROKER/Corbis; 14, © D. Robert & Lorri Franz/Corbis; 15, © Frank Fichtmueller/Alamy; 16, © Yvette Cardozo/Alamy; 17, © Leonard Rue Enterprises/Animals Animals/Earth Scenes; 18, © Quinton, Michael/Minden Pictures/National Geographic Creative; 19, © Illg, Gordon & Cathy/Animals Animals; 20, © McDonald Wildlife Photog./Animals Animals; 21, © Zoonar/Don Mammoser; 22A, © Fuse/Getty; 22B, © Arco Images GmBH/Alamy; 22C, © Daniel Webb/Getty; 22D, © Berquist, Paul & Joyce/Animals Animals; 22E, © David R. Frazier Photolibrary Inc./Alamy; 22F, © George H. H. Huey/Alamy; 22G, © Rosalie Kreulen/Shutterstock; 22H, © Nature Picture Library/Alamy; 23TL, © Geofferey Kuchera/Shutterstock; 23TM, © Anton Foltin/Shutterstock; 23TR, © Christian Colista/Shutterstock; 23BL, © Yvette Cardozo/Alamy; 23BM, © Arto Hakola/Shutterstock; 23BR, © Tom Walker/Visuals Unlimited/Corbis.

Publisher: Kenn Goin
Editor: Jessica Rudolph
Creative Director: Spencer Brinker
Design: Alix Wood
Photo Researcher: Michael Win

Library of Congress Cataloging-in-Publication Data

Goldish, Meish.
  Bobcat / by Meish Goldish.
     pages cm.—(Desert animals : searchin' for shade)
  Includes bibliographical references and index.
  ISBN 978-1-62724-538-8 (library binding)—ISBN 1-62724-538-3 (library binding)
  I. Bobcat—Juvenile literature. I. Title.
  QL737.C23G637 2014
  599.75'36—dc23
                              2014040705

For more information, write to Bearport Publishing Company, Inc., 45 West 21st Street, Suite 3B, New York, New York 10010. Printed in the United States of America.

10 9 8 7 6 5 4 3 2 1

Contents

Waiting for Sundown

It's a hot summer afternoon in the **desert**.

A bobcat rests in the shade under a bush.

The bobcat will wait for the sun to go down.

Then it will hunt for a meal in the cool, dark night.

desert

The bobcat is a member of the cat family. This group includes animals such as lions, tigers, mountain lions, and pet cats. The bobcat gets its name because of its short, or bobbed, tail.

bobbed tail

a bobcat resting in the shade

5

Staying Cool

Bobcats are found only in North America.

Besides deserts, they also live in forests and swamps and on mountains.

In the desert, temperatures can rise to more than 120°F (49°C).

During the hottest part of the day, bobcats find shady places to rest.

They stay cool inside **hollow** logs, under bushes, or in caves.

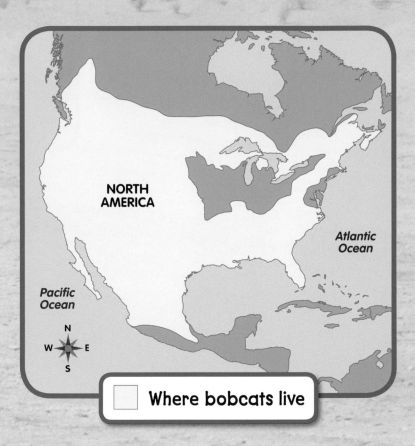

NORTH AMERICA

Atlantic Ocean

Pacific Ocean

N
W E
S

☐ Where bobcats live

What kinds of desert animals do you think bobcats eat?

A bobcat may find a different place to rest every day.

Desert Meals

Bobcats eat mostly meat.

They hunt many animals, including rabbits, squirrels, rats, birds, lizards, snakes, and deer.

Sometimes a bobcat will hunt **prey** by waiting in a hiding place on the ground.

When an animal gets close, the bobcat grabs it with its teeth or **claws**.

dead rabbit

A bobcat may also sit in a tall tree or cactus to wait for prey. When an animal walks by on the ground, the cat will leap on top of it.

Bobcat Foods

snake

squirrel

kangaroo rat

rabbit

lizard

Bobcats can hunt in another way. What do you think it is?

Silent Hunter

Sometimes a bobcat will hunt prey by walking quietly through the desert.

The bobcat has soft pads on the bottoms of its paws.

The soft pads let the cat follow an animal without making any noise.

As the bobcat hunts, it swivels its large ears backward and forward.

This helps it hear creatures that are moving along the ground.

large ears

When it's summer in the desert, bobcats usually hunt at night to avoid the daytime heat. In winter, when the desert is cooler, the cats may hunt during the day or night.

dead rat

A Deadly Leap

While the bobcat is walking, it may spot or hear a rabbit or other prey.

Then it crouches down and leaps up to 10 feet (3 m) into the air.

In an instant, the bobcat grabs the rabbit with its long, sharp claws.

The cat then sinks its razor-sharp teeth into the rabbit's neck to kill it.

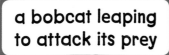

a bobcat leaping to attack its prey

Just before being attacked, an animal may not see or hear the bobcat. The prey is caught completely by surprise.

13

Keep Out!

Most of the time, a bobcat lives on its own.

Each adult bobcat has its own area in the desert where it hunts for food and rests.

This area is called its **territory**.

The bobcat uses its sharp claws to make scratch marks on trees.

The marks are a sign for other bobcats to keep out of its territory.

a bobcat making scratch marks on a fallen tree

A bobcat's desert territory may be as small as 1 square mile (2.6 sq km) or as large as 25 square miles (65 sq km). The size depends on how much prey is in the area. In places with less prey, the bobcat needs more land to hunt on.

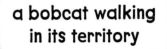
a bobcat walking in its territory

Sometimes, two bobcats will live together for a short period of time. Why do you think they do this?

Starting a Family

The only time the bobcat shares its space is when it is time to **mate**.

In fall or winter, a male and a female bobcat will spend several days together.

Then each cat goes off on its own.

Two months after mating, the female gives birth to one to six babies, called kittens.

female bobcat

male bobcat

During their time together, the male and female bobcats hunt and eat as a pair.

bobcat kittens

How do you think a mother bobcat cares for her babies?

Raising Babies

The mother cares for her kittens in a protected den, such as the inside of a cave or hollow log.

Safe in the den, the kittens drink their mother's milk.

When the babies are two months old, the mother leaves them for short periods of time.

She brings meat back to the den for the kittens to eat.

Soon, she teaches the kittens how to hunt.

bird

To teach her kittens to hunt, the mother brings live prey to them. She shows the babies how to kill an animal by biting its neck.

a mother bobcat
with her kittens

Leaving Home

As the bobcat kittens get bigger, they spend lots of time playing and exploring.

At the age of about ten months, they know how to hunt for themselves.

The young bobcats leave their mother.

They may travel more than 100 miles (161 km).

Then each bobcat finds a part of the desert to call its own!

bobcat kittens playing

Adult bobcats can grow up to 4 feet long (1.2 m) and weigh up to 30 pounds (13.6 kg). They usually live for 10 to 12 years.

Science Lab

Spot the Bobcat

Imagine you are a scientist who studies bobcats. Bobcats can live in the same areas as mountain lions, red foxes, and coyotes. These animals are often similar in shape or color.

mountain lion

red fox

coyote

bobcat

Scientists must be able to identify an animal—even if they only spot a little of the creature.

Which of these pictures shows a bobcat? What animal is shown in each of the other pictures?

A
B
C
D

(The answers are on page 24.)

Science Words

claws (KLAWZ) the sharp, curved nails on the feet of an animal

desert (DEZ-urt) dry land with little rainfall and few plants; some deserts are covered in sand

hollow (HOL-oh) empty on the inside

mate (MAYT) to come together in order to have young

prey (PRAY) an animal that is hunted by another animal for food

territory (TER-uh-tor-ee) the area where an animal lives and finds its food

Index

Read More

Randall, Henry. *Bobcats (Cats of the Wild).* New York: PowerKids Press (2011).

Shea, Therese. *Bobcats in the Dark (Creatures of the Night).* New York: Gareth Stevens (2013).

Squire, Ann. *Bobcats (True Book).* New York: Children's Press (2005).

Learn More Online

To learn more about bobcats, visit **www.bearportpublishing.com/DesertAnimals**

About the Author

Meish Goldish has written more than 200 books for children. His book *Surf Dog Miracles* was a Children's Choices Selection in 2014. He lives in Brooklyn, New York, where the Brooklyn Bobcats play in the Regional American Football League.

Answers for Page 22

- A is a coyote.
- B is a bobcat.
- C is a mountain lion.
- D is a red fox.